INTERIORS

poems by

Maura Stanton

Finishing Line Press
Georgetown, Kentucky

INTERIORS

These little boxes are for Olive and Oleander

ACKNOWLEDGMENTS

Artful Dodge: "Net"
Bateau: "Crack," "Stapler," "The Anonymous Mermaid"
Denver Quarterly: "Kaleidoscope"
Ecotone: "Global Warming"
Hayden's Ferry Review: "Magician's Hat"
Hotel Amerika: "Cartoon," "Pearl"
Matchbook: "Birthday Cake"
Mid-American Review: "Ship in a Bottle," "Trojan Horse"
New Ohio Review: "Tool Box," "Fortune Cookie," "Jonah"
Plume: "Cotton Candy"
Poetry East: "Bubble"
roger: "Turtle Tells All," "The Whale"
Salamander: "Under the Bed"
32 Poems: "Jigsaw Puzzle," "Matchbox," "Tornado"

Publisher: Leah Huete de Maines
Editor: Christen Kincaid
Cover Art: Maura Stanton
Author Photo: Richard Cecil
Cover Design: Elizabeth Maines McCleavy

Order online: www.finishinglinepress.com
also available on amazon.com

Author inquiries and mail orders:
Finishing Line Press
PO Box 1626
Georgetown, Kentucky 40324
USA

Table of Contents

Interior: 1. being within; inside of anything; internal, further toward a center. 2. of or pertaining to something within; 3. situated well inland from the coast or border 4. domestic 6. inner, private, secret
Random House Dictionary

TURTLE TELLS ALL

When we draw our heads inside, you don't exist
anymore. We hear you out there droning on about this
or that, taking notes or threatening something, but
we've gone back into our shells. The backs of our
shells all look alike, but inside each one is different.
Mine is currently baby blue with hexagonal patterns
and yellow highlights. Most days I'm out swimming,
but sometimes I trudge ashore looking for a good place
to lay some eggs. If I glimpse you coming my way or
if I even see one of your big footprints in the sand,
that's it. I pull inside. You won't hear a peep out of
me, even if you give me a hard kick, or pick me up and
turn me over and measure my belly. I seldom snap.
And it's not because I'm afraid of you. I just dislike
you. I prefer listening to the echoes of the latest sea
music in my shell, or repainting my dome in shades of
ocean. When you let me go, I wait patiently until I
can't hear your palaver anymore.

GLOBAL WARMING

He looks up from his magazine at the beach ball globe floating near the edge of the pool. The familiar pink and blue and yellow continents painted across turquoise seas look like harmless flowers; maybe if he gets inside the globe he can figure out what's wrong by studying the reverse sides of the cheerful landmasses. But he has to be quick before his kids start batting the ball around, so he squeezes through the plug at the top, falling down to the bottom and sprawling across the backside of the South Pole next to a dead fly. How did the fly get in here? He gets to his feet, looking up. From inside the globe, the topographies appear as flat, featureless clouds. It's hard to breathe, and when he starts climbing up the sticky plastic sides toward Australia, he's soon covered in sweat. It makes no difference whether he crosses an ocean or a country, there's no breeze, no mountains, no fish or trees, only the happy whoop of distant children and the insistent hiss of air leaking from the top.

PEARL

Something is bothering an oyster so it makes a pearl.
Instead of admiring the lustrous beauty, oohing and
aahing like everyone else, the homunculus is annoyed
by all the fuss. He decides to find the petty source of
the irritation. He gets out his tiny chisel and mallet
and starts hacking his way inside the pearl's nacre.
But as soon as he gets past one iridescent layer, he
finds himself up against the next one, cutting through
platelets of calcium carbonate and sheets of shiny
chitin. All around him the many colors of the
spectrum are being reflected in gorgeous waves. He
puts on sunglasses, shielding his eyes from rainbow
colors; and gloves, to avoid feeling the sensual silky
protein he's destroying bit by bit. Now he's getting
somewhere! The circles are smaller. And here's the
center. He pockets a grain of sand, planning his
triumphant return, a museum to display his tidbit, but
now he's trapped. The oyster has encysted him like
any other parasite and the pearl grows larger and even
lovelier.

STAPLER

You were born looking just like all the other silver staples, shaped like a [bracket] and attached to the others in a long row. The row was nestled inside a cardboard box with other rows that looked just like it. For a long time you waited for someone to open the box, dreaming about your fate. Maybe you were born to staple revolutionary scientific reports or vital government documents. Other rows were chosen. Then finally your row was lifted out and fitted down inside the stapler. The row broke into two pieces, and one staple fell out, hitting the floor with a sad ping, but the spring pressed the rest of you back together. Now you were number sixty in line. You felt a Wham. The first staple in your row stapled what it was destined to staple, and you jolted closer to the end. You were about to hold something together for the rest of your existence, and you tingled with joy. Now! Now! The stapler head slammed down. Eeek! It wasn't your fault that you went into the paper crooked. Nevertheless, you were plucked out and tossed into a waste can.

BIRTHDAY CAKE

She's been crouched in here a long time, wearing her
pasties and her G-string, waiting for the signal to jump
out of the cake. She's cramped and tired and worried
that she'll forget the special song she's suppose to
sing. And she's hungry! She keeps reaching up for
handfuls of sweet cake, stuffing it into her mouth.
Sounds outside the cake are muffled, but she can hear
the roar of laughter whenever somebody tells a smutty
joke. She imagines them all sitting around the table,
getting drunk. Occasionally the cake trembles when
somebody sticks their finger into the thick frosting for
a lick, or pulls off one of the sugar roses. What if they
forget she's in here and start slicing the cake with a big
knife? They might cut her head off! She'd better get
out of here. She wipes the crumbs off her lips. She
flexes the muscles in her calves, and springs up
through layers and layers of white and chocolate. She
flings out her arms. Happy Birthday! But they've all
gone into the other room to watch dirty movies.

TROJAN HORSE

It's dark in here. You can hear murmurs and footsteps as curious Trojans walk around the big wooden gift horse, tapping the belly, climbing up on the back. The officers hidden inside have a view through the hollow eyes, but you're just a foot soldier, and you're crouched down in one of the horse's legs, the left back leg to be exact. In fact, your rank is so low that you're really in the hoof, and several other soldiers are wedged above you, cursing and farting. When the Trojans start to pull the horse through the gates, the whole contraption shakes, and another soldier's bronze shield bangs your shoulder. A few hours later, the command to move out is whispered back through the ranks. You feel shifting above you, then the clank of armor as soldiers leap out the trap door in the side. Already the fight's begun. You hear the whoosh of spears, the thud of punctured livers. Is this what you were born for? You climb up the leg slowly, slowly, slowly.

MAGICIAN'S HAT

Once she was his assistant and wore a spangled outfit
with red high heels. Then one day she stepped into the
cabinet, where she used to temporarily disappear.
Only she didn't reappear this time. She found herself
stuck in his hat with the other tricks he didn't use
anymore. The lonely rabbits nuzzled her. The anxious
doves cooed in her ear. She leaned back against the
bouquet of paper flowers, which hadn't been
flourished for years, and held onto the long rope of silk
scarves, hoping to be pulled out. But he wasn't using
that trick anymore, either. She could hear the cymbals
crashing on stage, and the audience applauding his new
tricks. Once she stood on tiptoe and looked over the
black rim. She glimpsed the rhinestone bracelet of his
new assistant as she pushed her back. Then everything
was quiet for a long time. The next time she got up the
courage to peer out, the hat was sitting alone on a
dusty shelf.

TOOL BOX

Under the rusting red metal lid we're waiting for
you—your father's tools. We always knew you
weren't going to build a doghouse or repair the stairs
or tighten a bibcock faucet, but we wanted to be of use
as in the old days. Ah, the old days! When we heard
your father's tread on the basement steps, we were
thrilled. The hammer clenched its head, the bubble
trembled in the level, the pliers stretched its jaws. But
after your father died it was worse than we expected.
You carted us out to your car, left us for months in the
trunk, and then stuck us on the floor of this hall closet
next to the vacuum cleaner. Now the hacksaw's teeth
are rusting, the file's worn down, and the measuring
tape sags beside the plane. The poor jackscrew, no
longer attached to a work bench, has grown forgetful,
and thinks it's really a micrometer caliper. All you
care about is duct tape these days, tearing off flashy
shreds to cover your botched work while the tough
little nails languish. So watch out! All of us in here
are fed up with your disregard for some of mankind's
oldest inventions, so if you ever do open this lid you're
going to get hurt.

THE WHALE

What was it like in there? Jonah looks thoughtful.
Dark, is all he says at first, but when he's interviewed
by a local newspaper he points out that the whale's
stomach smelled terrible. *Well, not completely dark,*
he adds, when he gives the commencement speech at
his old high school. *You see the ribs arched over like,
like... like a cathedral, and the whale swallowed
some phosphorescent fish.* He's paid a lot of money to
write a magazine article in which he describes building
a bed out of abalone shells, and learning to appreciate
raw tuna. In his bestselling memoir he goes into detail
about the sloshing pools of acid that flooded the
stomach when it was digesting, threatening to dissolve
him, how he had to balance himself on a mound of
shark skulls. He played tiddlywinks with periwinkles,
he tells the audience on a talk show, getting a laugh.
He doesn't write the screenplay, but they fly him to
Hollywood as a consultant. CNN reports rumors that
he made everything up. He doesn't go to the premier.
He holes up in his apartment with the lights off eating
sardines with his fingers.

MATCHBOX

Once upon a time this matchbox was filled with fresh
wooden matches. Another cricket lived here for a
while. You found one of his dried legs in a crack. This
was right after a big hand scooped you up and put you
inside. At first you were busy testing your wings and
feet to make sure you hadn't been damaged. Then you
checked out the dimensions of the box, and tasted the
blades of grass provided for your dinner. You knew
you were expected to sing, that your life depended on
it, for if you were silent you'd be forgotten and no one
would feed you again or remember to release you. So
you strummed your feet merrily, and went through
your repertoire. You chanted and trilled and fiddled.
You sang about the green fields where you grew up,
and you imagined them listening to you with delight,
about to open the box. But no one ever did. You were
getting weaker. Crick, crick! You stuck one feeler up
through the slit at the end of the box, waving for help.
Oh, how ugly! somebody cried, throwing the matchbox
in the trash.

EGG SHELL

The egg that was a baby bird drained out long ago. She enters by the crack where there is still a little bit of dried gelatinous material that she has to pick away before she can get her head inside and pull herself through. She slides down. The walls are smooth and translucent, curving around her harmoniously. The texture of the shell varies between gritty and slippery but she manages to keep her balance as she walks to the end. The light keeps changing. It's bright and then it's pale. She hears whispers and murmurs outside as insects crawl through the grass around the shell. Her eyes grow used to the soft light and she sits down and leans back against the curved wall. She takes a deep breath of the subtle air. This is her life. There is nothing here but calm and pale blue space. She looks up and makes guesses about the shadows crossing the dome. That's the thorax of an ant, that's a waving blade of grass, that's a rose petal quickly blown off, and, oh no!! that's the rubber sole of a shoe about to step down and crush the shell.

SHIP IN A BOTTLE

For a long time he just admires his ship, the billowing
sails, the intricate rigging, the polished decks, the fine
brass wheel, the captain's cabin with it's bow window
and astrolabe. The hold is stocked with fine wines,
and the crew seems cheerful. The cook is always
baking cherry pies, and the swabbing sailors whistle as
they lug their buckets out for another day of washing
and polishing. He walks around with his hands behind
his back, looking out at the glass wall that protects him
from weather and seasickness. He used to puzzle over
the mystery of how the ship got into the bottle, but
now he wonders where the ship is headed. He started
out on a shelf in a library, but he was hoping to reach
the Azores, the rainy Hyades, or even Tahiti. He takes
out his spy glass but he keeps seeing the same horizon,
rows and rows of books. His hair is getting grey.
When he looks up, he doesn't see stars, only dust
falling like snow on the top of the bottle.

COTTON CANDY

At first it gives like a sponge, elastically, and you think
you'll only make an impression and get pushed back.
But then the web of spun sugar wilts a little from the
heat of your body, allowing you to sink softly into the
pink cloud. Your weight does the rest and now you're
really pushing through. Handfuls of the stuff turn into
tough strands under your sweating palms and feet.
You swing back and forth, enjoying yourself, glad you
decided to do this at last, but you're starting to notice
that the walls melt if you don't keep moving. You
climb higher and higher, your mouth full of sweet bits,
hoping you don't bump into the paper cone in the
center. The texture keeps changing, sometimes open
and lacy, other times tightly interknit. You admire the
delicate shades of rose and mauve, but you're aware of
a few unsightly knots of unspun sugar, or are those
gnats caught in the sticky web? Now there's a patch
above you that looks wet. A mouth is eating down to
you, the greedy lips puckering and sucking.

JONAH

Whoops! He was afraid this was going to happen.
He's been sucked up. The strong wind pulls him in
against the stiff fringe of the brush attachment, where
he gasps and tangles with bits of debris, strands of hair,
crumbs, dust bunnies, specks, soot, and flecks of
dander. The brush is swiped across the carpet, freeing
him from the tough indifferent bristles. He flies up the
silver tube, but since he's heavier than the rest of the
grime, he gets to catch his breath at the bend, pinned
against the cold metal until he's slapped free by a
dancing paperclip. Swoop! Suck! Up he goes into the
flexible plastic hose. Now and then he catches on the
accordion folds, but the air is warmer now, and he
feels himself being pulled closer and closer to the
engine thrumming in the center. Why, this isn't so
bad. He almost feels excited as he approaches his
destination, the special paper bag fitted inside the
machine where all the dirt in the house congregates.
And then he's in! He's dragged through the opening.
It's all over. There's nothing to do but make a cozy
nest in the mound of familiar filth.

UNDER THE BED

The cats have already clawed the covering off the bottom of the box spring mattress so when you decide not to go to work that Monday morning, it's an easy matter to crawl under the bed and up through the rip in the cloth. Now you're in a field of metal coils planted along rows of wooden slats. The coils disappear into the bunting sky above, each one twisted and bent like the trunks of ancient olive trees, no two alike. You can tell by bits of fur and dander that the cats used to sleep on the sagging cover between the slats, but their weight dragged it down. You keep your balance on the slats, admiring the strong coils that have held you up night after night, rising and compressing as you tossed and turned. But just as you congratulate yourself on finding a clever hiding place where the boss will never find you, the coils squeak and squeeze tightly together, forcing you to duck and crawl on all fours. You can hardly breathe. Somebody is sleeping on your bed.

THE ANONYMOUS MERMAID

I live in a big clamshell down here under the coral reef,
and I don't go out much anymore. You see, I used to
think I was special, with my flashy tail and perfect
breasts. Blue-green, green-blue, aqua marine—my
scales glittered, and I clamped shells in my long hair
and swam besides boats singing in a gorgeous voice.
Then I noticed something eerie. All mermaids looked
just like me. Some of us had bluer or greener tails, or
wore pink or white pearl necklaces, but it was hard to
tell us apart. And our songs were so similar, full of
sadness and verve, little bittersweet lyrics. A prince
might fall in love with this one or that one. It didn't
matter. We weren't getting anywhere. So I dived
down here, found this empty clamshell, and decorated
it with seaweed tapestries and sponge lounge chairs. I
made myself a pair of isinglass spectacles, borrowed
some squid ink, and began to compose an epic.

KALEIDOSCOPE

She used to think it would be fun to be a piece of
colored glass at the end of a child's kaleidoscope, a
tiny part of a bright pattern that shifted every time the
amazed kid turned the ring and looked through the
eyepiece, but now that she's in here, a gleaming glass
bead, she's not so sure. Whee! Here they go again!
The little beads shake and shimmer against the mirrors,
and another gorgeous symmetrical design appears, but
she's beginning to have trouble telling herself apart
from the reflections of herself. Is she really up here or
down there? Of course it doesn't matter, she tells
herself, it's the overall impression that counts. . . and
now she's spinning again, bumping against other glass
beads, part of a new arrangement, and she tells herself
she should be proud to be a representative of
ephemeral beauty. But why is the kid shaking the
kaleidoscope like that? Now he's banging it against
the wall. One of the mirrors breaks. The glass beads
spill out, and she rolls under the bed next to a dusty M
& M.

FORTUNE COOKIE

6 a.m. It's cold and raining and you don't want to get out of bed. It's one of those days when you'd like to stay home from work, curled up somewhere comfortable and nice with your knees against your chest. Why not inside a fortune cookie? And at once you imagine yourself inside the sweet crispy shell, the paper fortune wrapped around your body like a sheet. You're about to close your eyes and go back to sleep when you start to worry about the fortune. Is this one of those really good fortunes like the one you've kept in your wallet for years, *You will never need to worry about a steady income?* Or is it more sinister like the one you pulled out last month, *Idleness is the holiday of fools.* You want to read your fortune but you've got to break out of the cookie shell. Only you can't. You're paralyzed. This is someone else's fortune cookie, and you've got to wait patiently until they pour the tea, and crack it open. Then they'll laugh and read your fortune out loud for everyone to hear, *Your problem lies not in a lack of ability but in a lack of ambition.*

CRACK

He's not sure what kind of crack he's fallen into. If he's fallen into a sofa crack, then somebody might stick a hand down between the crushed velvet cushions and pull him out along with a dime and a nickel, delighted to find him. But they might just as easily use the hose on a vacuum cleaner and never even see him as he whooshes up the tube. He could have fallen into a crack in the pavement, which would account for all the shoes that seem to be walking indifferently above him. Or this crack could be a fissure in a house. The predicted earthquake might cause a real break, and expose him to view, but he could also be plastered over and hidden forever. He knows he ought to accept his crack and start exploring the narrow space he's been given, find out if anything else is in here besides dust and cockroach legs. Instead, he puts on his sunglasses and makes yet another futile attempt to climb toward the light that shines far, far above him, trying to pull himself out even as he starts to slip back.

SKELETON IN THE CLOSET

I've been in here so long I think you've forgotten about me. At first, I'd rattle my bones every time you opened the door, but you couldn't distinguish me from the clack of hangers. When I tried leaning forward a little, you pushed me into the broken umbrellas on the top shelf as if you didn't see me. And, hey, maybe you didn't. I disguised myself under your winter coat, but that was the year you bought a new one, and I got shoved to the back with ski jackets and stained parkas. I devised clever ways to get your attention, but you never felt me grasping your finger bones when you put on your warm gloves, or noticed how I chilled your hat with my skull. Sometimes I wore your boots or wrapped a scarf around my neck, hoping you'd shriek, but you'd reach right past me for a fleece jacket. So I slunk back here, brooding, hunched in your old trench coat. Am I invisible? No, my ribs shimmer, my tibia glow, my spine phosphoresces. I vow to keep jumping out at you, knowing that someday you'll finally recognize my friendly grin.

BUBBLE

You're not sure how you got into this bubble but you
aren't complaining. Your bubble is transparent, but if
you focus near instead of far, you can see the rainbow
colors of the curved walls. You walk around on the
bottom of the bubble, bouncing, looking down through
your feet at the backyard below. You see the head of a
child down there, blowing more bubbles through a
wand, but the other bubbles that float up near you seem
to be empty, and you think that's a shame. It's
wonderful inside a bubble. When you jump, the
rubbery substance sinks delightfully, and then propels
you higher than you expected; you effervesce for a
moment, before touching down gently on the invisible
floor of the bubble. You're above the treetops now.
The ride is gentle. You lie back and rest your head
against the film of the bubble, looking up at the clouds.
How long will this last? You don't want to know,
even though you can already hear the diving blue jay,
the killer bees, the big red Frisbee sailing your
direction.

CARTOON

Are you stuck in a single box, or are you part of a narrative strip? Someone's drawn you with big round eyes, stick legs and arms, and given you a torso shaped like a light bulb. You have floppy feet and droopy arms and curlicue hair. You're the only one in this frame, but you have the impression that other characters in other frames are preparing to hit you or bop you or pull something on you. But maybe you're just paranoid. The next box over may have nothing to do with your story. You wish you could read the balloon over your head, or the caption down below, but you're not on the same plane. You stretch out your arms. The lines on either side of you feel rubbery, as if they might give, allowing you to break out, but though you push with all your might you can't bend them. Ah, somebody's reading the newspaper. You feel eyes focused on your funny body. Your mouth is shaped in a big O. You know you're screaming, but you can't hear anything except chuckling, followed by rustling. The reader is already turning the page.

JIGSAW PUZZLE

You're not one of the border pieces because you don't have a straight edge. You're an irregular inner piece with a bulbous protrusion at one end. You've been dumped into the top of the puzzle box with a lot of other pieces, waiting your turn to be fitted into the big picture. The border pieces got taken out first. You hoped you might be next, but the puzzle maker flicked you aside to look for some pretty blue pieces for the sky. Next came the white pieces, followed by the green pieces. You and the other drab brown and grey pieces are in the majority but because you're all cut in similar shapes, it's hard to tell you apart. Are you earth or a piece of rock or a shadow? Using your puny strength, you shift and slide away from the others, and finally you're noticed and picked up. You've never been so excited. Where do you go? The puzzle maker tries to press you here and there, but your bulbous protrusion doesn't fit into the mountains or the seashore. You're a real problem. Annoyed, the puzzle maker sweeps the whole unfinished puzzle back into the box.

TORNADO

She's running down the street, hoping to get home
before a storm breaks, when a tornado dips down on
top of her. She's drawn up by her long hair. She's
been afraid of tornados all her life and now here she is,
inside her worst nightmare, a dark space with whirling
walls. She's going to die. Centrifugal force keeps her
from falling out. She wishes she could close her eyes
but she can't. She looks down. The tornado races
away from town and across dark sodden fields. Then it
makes a sudden scoop. She hears a loud moo, and a
cow flies up, along with some daisies. The cow begins
to nibble the daisies as if nothing had happened. Then
she notices that lots of stuff is pinned inside the
tornado, stuff she could use. She edges sideways
against the wall of wind and grabs a glass. The cow
gives her milk. She finds a clothesline. Now she has
things to wear. When she spots a bed, she lies down.
She has no idea where she's going, but she might as
well make herself comfortable.

NET

And you're not even edible! But you got caught in the net with all the others and now you feel them wildly thrashing around and around, scraping you with their glittery scales and slapping you with their desperate flashing tails. You're somewhere in the middle, thousands above you, thousands below you. It isn't fair. You're flesh is stringy and bitter, you're dun-colored and lumpy, with an ugly snout. You've always minded your own business, stuck to the muddy bottom, ignored the sleek schools and bright fins darting insouciantly through the waves. You never asked for anything. You're a survivor! So how could this happen? You squirm and butt your way through the terrified mass, hoping you can reach the top or the sides or the bottom and tear open a hole. Baby crabs, sensing your determination, clip themselves to your caudal fin. Yes, yes, you're going to make it! You grunt and shove. But already you feel the big tug as the net is lifted out of the water, up, up into the tasteless strangling air.

Maura Stanton's first book of poetry, *Snow On Snow*, was selected by Stanley Kunitz for the Yale Series of Younger Poets Award, and published in 1975. She has published five other books of poetry, *Cries of Swimmers* (Utah 1984), *Tales of the Supernatural* (Godine 1988), *Life Among the Trolls* (Carnegie Mellon 1998), *Glacier Wine* (Carngeie Mellon 2002) and *Immortal Sofa* (University of Illinois 2008) as well as a novel and three books of short stories. Her poems and stories have appeared in *Southwest Review, Antioch Review, The Atlantic, The New Yorker, Poetry, Southern Poetry Review, New England Review, Gettysburg Review, River Styx, American Poetry Review, The Yale Review, The Hudson Review* and many other magazines and anthologies.

A graduate of the University of Minnesota and the Iowa Writers' Workshop, she has won two fellowships from the National Endowment for the Arts, an O'Henry Award, the Richard Sullivan Prize in Short Fiction from the University of Notre Dame Press, the Michigan Literary Fiction Award for Short Story, the Supernatural Fiction Award from the Ghost Story.com and the Nelson Algren Award from *The Chicago Tribune*. Her poems have been featured on *The Writer's Almanac, Poetry Daily* and the BBC radio program *Words and Music*. Her O'Henry Award winning short story, "Oh Shenandoah," was read at Symphony Space in New York City and at the Dallas Art Museum as part of Selected Shorts celebration of 100 Years of the O'Henry Awards. She lives in Bloomington, Indiana with her husband, the poet Richard Cecil.